Chao Phya Thipakon, Henry Alabaster

The modern Buddhist

Chao Phya Thipakon, Henry Alabaster

The modern Buddhist

ISBN/EAN: 9783742891280

Manufactured in Europe, USA, Canada, Australia, Japa

Cover: Foto ©Thomas Meinert / pixelio.de

Manufactured and distributed by brebook publishing software
(www.brebook.com)

Chao Phya Thipakon, Henry Alabaster

The modern Buddhist

THE MODERN BUDDHIST;

BEING

THE VIEWS OF A SIAMESE MINISTER OF STATE ON
HIS OWN AND OTHER RELIGIONS.

TRANSLATED, WITH REMARKS, BY

HENRY ALABASTER,

INTERPRETER OF H.B.M. CONSULATE-GENERAL IN SIAM.

LONDON:

TRÜBNER & CO., 60, PATERNOSTER ROW.

1870.

THE MODERN BUDDHIST.

OF the three hundred and sixty-five millions of men, the third of the human race who, according to a common estimate, profess in some form the religion of Buddha, the four million inhabitants of Siam are excelled by none in the sincerity of their belief and the liberality with which they support their religion. No other Buddhist country, of similar extent, can show so many splendid temples and monasteries. In Bangkok alone there are more than a hundred monasteries, and, it is said, ten thousand monks and novices. More than this, every male Siamese, some time during his life, and generally in the prime of it, takes orders as a monk and retires for some months or years to practise abstinence and meditation in a monastery.

B

The principal works on Buddhism in our language are uninviting to the general reader. The most able translators have not been able to render the Buddhist classics anything but tedious to read, and it is seldom that the great authorities go beyond the classics. Such pleasing and instructive discourses as Max Müller's late lecture on Buddhistic Nihilism are rare indeed, and the most familiar accounts of Buddhism depict it surrounded by, and almost buried in the mass of superstitions which have been from time to time connected with it.

Such treatment is no more fair than it would be fair to describe Christianity as inseparable from every monkish fable which has from time to time found credence. Indeed, it is still less fair, for Christianity has always had some check kept on alterations of its teachings, by the fact that some of its earliest apostles committed their views to writing, but Buddhism having, for upwards of four hundred years,* from the days when Somana Kodom or Buddha

* Buddhists themselves say four hundred and fifty years, but this is improbable. Some modern scholars are inclined to believe that the period was much less.

first taught it, been transmitted by oral tradition alone, must, in the very nature of things, have been overwhelmed with ideas which were not those of its founder.

Our object is to show something of the religion of Buddha apart from its grosser superstitious surroundings, not by our own analysis, but by extracts from the writings of a thoughtful Siamese Buddhist on his own and other religions.

Somdet Phra Paramendr Maha Mongkut, the late King of Siam, has been called the founder of a new school of Buddhist thought, having, while himself a monk, eminent among monks for his knowledge of the Buddhist Scriptures, boldly preached against the canonicity of those of them whose relations were opposed to his reason, and his knowledge of modern science. His Majesty was a man of remarkable genius and acquirements. His powers as a linguist were considerable, and enabled him to use an English library with facility. Had he been able to publish his ideas at a late period of his life, we might have had still more enlightenment shown, than appears in the book we are about to present to

our readers; but his position as King was a
bar to his doing such a thing; he could do no
more than in some measure inspire his minister,
whose ideas were less advanced.

The Bangkok Calendar, an annual published
in Siam, contains some notes on the life of the
late monarch, some careful descriptions of
Buddhist observances, and translations of
Buddhist works, and we shall find it convenient to quote at times from its pages, especially in our references to the 'Traiphoom,' or
Buddhist cosmogony, of which it gives a convenient abstract.

Chao Phya Thipakon, better known to
foreigners as Chao Phya Praklang, successfully
conducted the foreign affairs of Siam from
1856, when Sir John Bowring's Treaty opened
the country to foreign trade, until two years
ago, when he retired into private life stricken
with blindness. The minister was greatly
esteemed by those his duties brought him in
contact with; he was always open to argument, and never let anything disturb the cour-
teous urbanity of his demeanour. It was his
wont, when with those who could converse
freely in Siamese, to end every official inter-

view with a private discussion on some theoretical or transcendental subject, therein differing from all the other leading men in his country, whose thoughts and inquiries were always about material, mechanical, and practical subjects. For instance, if gunpowder was alluded to, he would expatiate on the advantage civilized nations derived from it, or would speculate on its combustion changing a solid into gas, while any other nobleman would have discussed either the best proportion of its ingredients, or the best place to buy it, and the right price to pay for it.

By many years of verbal inquiry, and by reading the elementary tracts published by missionaries in Siam, he acquired such knowledge as he has of European science and of foreign religions.

The results of his speculations he published two years ago in the ' Kitchanukit,' " A book explaining many things," which, independently of its internal qualities, is curious, as being the first book printed and published by a Siamese without foreign assistance. He thus states his reason for becoming an author :—

" I propose to write a book for the instruction of the young, being of opinion that the course of teaching at present followed in the temples is unprofitable. That course consists of the spelling-book, religious formulæ, and tales. What knowledge can any one gain from such nonsense as 'O Chan, my little man, please bring rice and curry nice, and a ring, a copper thing round my little brother's arm to cling'? jingling sound without sense,—a fair example of a large class of reading exercise. I shall endeavour to write fruitfully on various subjects, material knowledge and religion, discussing the evidence of the truth and falsity of things. The young will gain more by studying this than by reading religious formulæ and novels, for they will learn to answer questions that may be put to them. My book will be one of questions and answers, and I shall call it 'a book explaining many things.'"

We can, from our own experience, confirm the character thus given to the education of children in monasteries, which are the only extensive educational establishments in Siam. The pupils who remain long enough in them, learn to read and to write their own language, and also, if clever, the Pali language in the Kawm, or old Cambodian character; but when the language is mastered, the literature it opens to them is for the most part silly and unprofitable. To quote again from our author:—

"Our Siamese literature is not only scanty but nonsensical, full of stories of genii stealing women, and men fighting with genii, and extraordinary persons who could fly through the air, and bring dead people to life. And even those works which profess to teach anything, generally teach it wrong, so that there is not the least profit, though one studies them from morning to night."

The work, though mainly devoted to the comparison of Buddhism with other religions, commences with an account of native and foreign methods of reckoning time, the construction of calendars, the author's views on astronomy, the nature of air and water, etc., prefaced by the modest remark,

"Though I may be wrong, still, what I write will serve to stimulate men's thoughts, and lead to their finding out the truth."

It seems to us that much of this is inserted for the purpose of showing that the absurd cosmogony of the 'Traiphoom,' a work which the old school of Buddhists regard as sacred, is not wholly an essential part of the Buddhist religion; but that of Somana Kodom, or Buddha, even if it did not teach the truths of modern science, taught nothing opposed to them. It is also written, to keep in some degree the promise of the first page, that it shall be a book of education for the young, a book about many things. It is not until the author has warmed to his work that the religious and controversial element takes the place of every other.

It is not our purpose to refer much to this first part of the book. There is a great deal of useful information in it, strangely mixed up with nonsense. The author has been at times deliberately deceived by his informants, and gravely quotes some very foolish stories which there is no use in repeating. We prefer to give, as an example of his style, a part of his discourse on rain.

"Now as to the cause of the dry and wet seasons, I will first give the explanation as it stands in the 'Traiphoom.' When the sun goes south near the heavenly abode of the Dewa Wasawalahok, the Lord of Rain, the Dewa finds it too hot to move out of his palace, and so it is dry season. But when the sun is in the north, out he goes and sets the rain falling.

"Another statement is that in the Himaphan forest there is a great lake, named Anodat, and that a certain kind of wind sucks up its waters and scatters them about. Another statement is, that Phya Nak,* when playing, blows water high up into the air, where it is caught by the wind and falls as rain. There is no proof of these stories and I have no faith in them, for I cannot see where Wasawalahok lives, and I don't know whether he can make rain fall or not. As for the wind sucking up the water in the Himaphan forest, that forest lying to the north, all clouds must needs form in the north, but as in fact they form at all points of the compass, how can we say they come from Himaphan? As for the Nak playing with water, no one has seen him, so there is no proof of it. The Chinese say rain falls because the Dewas will it, or because the Dragon shows his might by sucking up the sea water, which by his power becomes fresh. They

* The King of the Naks—hooded serpents of immense size and power.

having seen that in the open ocean a wind sometimes sucks up the water transparently into the sky, and that thence arise clouds, believe that the Dragon does it. There is no proof of this. The Brahmins, and other believers in God the Creator, believe that He makes the rain to fall, that men may cultivate their fields and live. I cannot say whether God does this or not, for it seems to me that if so, He would of His great love and mercy make it fall equally all over the earth, so that all men might live and eat in security. But this is not the case,—indeed, in some places no rain falls for years together, the people have to drink brackish water, and cannot cultivate their lands, or have to trust but to the dew to moisten them; besides, a very great deal of the rain falls on the seas, the mountains, and the jungles, and does no good to man at all. Sometimes too much falls, flooding the towns and villages, and drowning numbers of men and animals, sometimes too little falls in the plains for rice to be grown, while on the mountain tops rain falls perpetually through seasons wet and dry. How can it be said that God, the creator of the world, causes rain, when its fall is so irregular? We now come to the idea of philosophers, who have some proof of their theory. They say rain falls somewhere every day without fail; for the earth, the sky, and the sea are like a still, and it is a property of salt water to yield fresh by distillation. The heat of the sun draws up steam from the sea and wherever there is moisture. Do not pools dry up? This steam is not lost, it flies to cool places above, and collecting in the cold skies becomes solid like ice, then when the hot season arrives this ice melts and forms into clouds, floating according to the wind, and when a wind forces a cloud near the earth, the hills and earth act on it like a magnet, draw it down, and there is rain. Hence it arises that rain water is cooler than other water, for it is formed by melting ice, and wherever the sun goes there it is rainy season."

We also give his remarks on epidemic diseases, which, like the preceding passage, illustrate his idea of the perfect equality that should result from Divine justice.

"How is it that in some years fevers prevail, in others not; in some ophthalmia, smallpox, etc., arise as epidemics, and in some animals are attacked by epidemics?

"Those who believe in devils say they cause it. Those who believe in God the Creator say He inflicts them as a punishment. The Mahometans say that there are trees in heaven, on each of whose leaves is the name of a human being, and whenever one of these leaves withers and falls the man whose name it bears dies with it. Old Siamese sages held that Phya Nak mixed poison with the air. Those who do not believe in devils ascribe epidemic diseases to the change of seasons, the change from heat to cold and cold to heat, disturbing the body which is healthy enough when the season is well set in and become thoroughly hot, or cold, or rainy, as is the case. They further say, the evil element in the atmosphere is a poisonous gas, affecting all those whose bodily state cannot resist its entry. Epidemics among animals can be accounted for by the poisonous gas finding an affinity for the elements of the animals. I find corroboration in the fact that exposure to bad air brings on sicknesses which those who remain sheltered do not suffer from. Moreover, the sea water,

which is a coarse atmosphere, when it is dis-
coloured and stinking kills the fish which are
in it, but those which are strong enough to
swim out of the foul part escape. The same
is seen with fish in a basin, which die if fresh
water is not given to them. So we find many
people live to old age without having the
smallpox, by always running away from any
place where it has broken out. In the same
way outbreaks of fever are local, and danger
is escaped by moving to another locality where
there is none. Now if it was a visitation of
God, there would be no running away from it.
I leave you to form your own opinion whether
it is the work of devils, or the visitation of
God, or the result of the fall of the leaves in
heaven, or of Phya Nak's poison, or of a bad
atmosphere."

The tides he explains by "lunar attraction,
which can be demonstrated by mathematics,
and is a more reasonable idea than that of the
Brahmins, some of whom believe that they
are caused by winds blowing back the water
in estuaries, and others that they are caused
by flames rising from time to time up a chim-
ney in the middle of the ocean, and forcing the
water back towards the coasts and rivers."

We shall now compare our author's view of the probable manner of formation of mountains and islands, with the account given in the 'Traiphoom' of the coming into being of a new group of worlds. First our author's view.

"It is said in our old books that the world arose from rain-water, which, drying up, left the earth floating about over it like a lotus-leaf, and the hills were caused by the water boiling up. The earth was left heaped irregularly, like rice at the bottom of a boiling rice-pot, and in time the higher parts became rock. Some think that the world was created by Allah for the use and advantage of mankind, but I cannot believe it, when I think of the terrible rocks on which ships are wrecked, and of fiery mountains, which are certainly not an advantage to man. How, then, can we ascribe it to a Creator? Those who say the higher parts became rock, do not say how they became so. Philosophers think that when the earth first formed there was fire beneath the surface, and that hills are due to that cause. And it is observed in other countries, as well as our own, that mountains and islands generally lie either in groups or in lines.

"And there is an inference of fire to be drawn from the fact that we can melt earth with fire, and it will become like rock or glass. I mention this only as a suggestion, for if the fire existed when the earth was formed, it should exist now; but no one has seen any hills arise in this way, and no one saw the world come into existence, so we cannot say anything for certain."

The 'Traiphoom' view is, that the whole of space has been for ever occupied by an infinite number of Chakrawans, or groups of worlds, all exactly similar, and each embracing a world of men, with a series of heavens and hells, etc. From time to time a billion of these groups are annihilated by fire, water, or wind, and a void remains, until the necessity of giving scope to merit and demerit,* causes the void to be again filled. First there appears an impalpable mist, gradually changing to an immense rainfall, continuing until a great part of the void is filled with water.

---

* The subject of " merit" and " demerit" is treated of later in the book. See pp. 58, *seq.*

Then arises a whirlwind, which shapes the
system, and dries up part of the water, causing
the mountains and plains to appear in slow
succession. During this time the only inhabitants of the system are the Phroms, the
highest order of angels, glorious beings, whose
own radiance illuminates the system, who need
no food, and have no sensual feelings. These
Phroms have, in the course of thousands of
previous transmigrations in pre-existing worlds,
gradually improved, until reaching that angelic state which is next to perfection. They
have then degenerated, and some will con-
tinue to degenerate until they reach the most
unhappy forms of life. Their degeneracy com-
menced by one of them craving for food, and
being so pleased on tasting it, that he could
not refrain from continually eating thenceforth. Others followed his example. Their
glory and luminosity left them, and by de-
grees, gluttony being followed by other desires, the distinction of sex arose, their forms
decreased in beauty, and they became human,
then brutal, and lastly devilish.

We revert to our modern Buddhist. Eclipses,
comets, meteors, and will-o'-the-wisps are in

turn treated of mainly according to European ideas, and the common Siamese idea of the intervention of spirits is ridiculed; but he claims that the theory of eclipses being caused by the dragon Phra Rahu swallowing the sun or moon, may be regarded as a parable veiling the truth; and he makes the somewhat bold statement that the great noise made in his country whenever there is an eclipse, the frantic beating of gongs and firing of guns, is not an effort on his countrymen's part to frighten the dragon, and make him drop the sun from his jaws, but is a sign of the joy of all men that their mathematicians are able to predict the time of such extraordinary events. This ingenious explanation seems more like a saying of the late King than that of the author of this book, and was probably the plea by which his Majesty justified himself for allowing his cannons to be fired on these occasions.

He fully adopts the general views of astronomy he has learnt from Europeans, even to the theory of the plurality of solar systems, and then imagines the question put, " Is not this contrary to the teaching of Buddha?" His argument in reply is lengthy, comprising

c

firstly, an abstract of the 'Traiphoom' cosmography; secondly, an account of the chief
religions of the world, which, he argues, were
all as opposed to true astronomical teaching as
Buddhism is supposed to be; and, thirdly, an
exposition of what he considers to be Buddha's
teaching on the subject, from which he de-
duces that Buddha knew the truth, and that
the 'Traiphoom' and other books of the class
are uncanonical. His abstract of the 'Traiphoom' cosmography, being intended for those
who have already read that book, is not very
definite; we shall therefore give our own in its
place.

The universe consists of an infinite number
of Chakrawans, each having a central mountain, Phra Men or Meru, surrounded by eight
belts of ocean, separated by seven annular
mountains, the nearest of which mountain is
Yukunthon. Outside of all, distant from the
seventh ring five million miles, is the annular
crystal mountain, Kow Chakrawan, 820,000
miles high, the boundary of the system. Si-
tuated on the inner belt of ocean, between
Meru and Yukunthon, are four groups of islands. The group to the south is that in-

habited by man; the groups to the north, the east, and the west, are inhabited by beings akin to men, but differing in appearance. On the annular mountains, and on and above Meru, are nineteen tiers of heavens or angelic worlds, the six lowest inhabited by Dewas, or ordinary angels; the nine above them by Phroms, or superior angels, having form; and the four above them by the highest class of angels, Phroms, without form. The Sun and Moon are Dewas, or angels living in gold and silver palaces, who travel round and round the Yukunthon mountains. Beneath the earth, at a distance of one hundred miles, is the nearest of eight places of misery, or hells. The whole system is held up by fish floating in an ocean, which is supported in space by wind. When these fish wag their tails, the earth trembles with an earthquake. In the 'Traiphoom' this system is elaborated with subdivisions of heavens and hells, and most tedious measurements of everything and place referred to.

It will be convenient for awhile to omit our author's account of the great religions of the world, excepting so far as bears on the point of astronomy. He first gives the Brahminical

cosmography, which closely resembles that in
the 'Traiphoom,' differing only in that it
names a creating God as the cause. He then
traces from Brahminism the religions of Abraham, Christ, and Mahomet, asking where any
of these teachers taught astronomy correctly,
and sums up in the following words :—

"When philosophers found out the truth,
the disciples of Mahomet put them in prison
because they taught that which was opposed
to the teaching of 'the Exact One,' which
made out the world to be a plain, with the
sun and moon revolving about it, much as our
'Traiphoom' does. But after a while, there
being too many witnesses of the truth of what
the philosophers asserted, they then adopted
their ideas, and incorporated them into their
religion. The ancients, whether Brahmins
or Arabs, or Jews or Chinese, or Europeans,
had much the same idea of cosmography, and
their present ideas on the subject were the
work of scientific men in modern times."

We now come to the third point, what was
Buddha's teaching on astronomy.

"When the Lord Buddha was born in the
land of the Brahmins, he knew all that was

just, and how to deliver the body from all ills.
This he knew perfectly. And he journeyed
and taught in Brahmin countries, the sixteen
great cities, for forty-five years, desiring only
that men should do right, and live suitably,
so that they might escape sorrow, and not be
subject to further changes of existence. Those
who have studied Pali know that the Lord
taught concerning the nature of life, and the
characteristics of good and evil, but never discoursed about cosmography. It is probable
that he knew the truth, but his knowledge
being opposed to the ideas of the 'Traiphoom,'
which every one then believed in, he said nothing about it. For if he had taught that the
world was a revolving globe, contrary to the
traditions of the people, who believed it to
be flat, they would not have believed him,
and might have pressed him with questions
about things of which there was no proof, except his allegations ; and they, disagreeing
with him, might have used towards him evil
language, and incurred sin. Besides, if he
had attacked their old traditions, he would
have stirred up enmity, and lost the time he
had for teaching all living beings. Therefore

he said nothing about cosmography. When a certain man asked him about it, he forbade him to inquire; he would not teach it himself, and forbade his disciples to speak of it., This can be seen in various Soodras; and where there are references to heaven and earth and hell in the sacred books, I presume they have found their way in as illustrations, etc. Yet there is an expression in those old books pointing out the truth for future men as to the revolution of the earth. The Pali expression is Wattakoloko, which, translated, is 'revolving world'; and those who did not know this translation explained it as referring to the sun and moon turning round the world, because they did not fully comprehend it. After the religion of Buddha had spread abroad, a certain king, desiring to know the truth as to cosmogony, inquired of the monks, and they knowing the omniscience of Buddha, and yet fearing that if they said Buddha never taught this, people would say 'your Lord is ignorant, and admired without reason,' took the ancient Scriptures, and various expressions in the Soodras and parables, and fables and proverbs, and connecting them together into a book, the

'Traiphoom,' produced it as the teaching of Buddha. The people of those days were uneducated and foolish, and believed that Buddha had really taught it ; and if any doubted, they kept their doubts to themselves, because they could not prove anything.

" Had the Lord Buddha taught cosmography as it is in the ' Traiphoom,' he would not have been omniscient, but by refraining from a subject which men of science were certain eventually to ascertain the truth of, he showed his omniscience."

Our author, nevertheless, will not give up the tradition that Buddha visited the heaven called Daodungsa, and there taught the angels. He believes that omnipotence may be gained by perfect virtue, abstinence, and thought, and does not think it impossible that it should enable a man to visit the starry heavens.

" It cannot be asserted that the Lord did not preach in Daodungsa, any more than the real existence of Mount Meru can be asserted. I have explained about this matter of Meru, and the other mountains, as an old tradition. But with respect to the Lord preaching on Daodungsa as an act of grace to his mother, I

believe it to be true, and that one of the many
stars or planets is the Daodungsa world. The
Lord Buddha disappeared for a period of three
months, and then returned. Had he been
hiding, that he might pretend he had been
preaching to the angels in heaven, he would
have been seen by somebody, and could not
have kept quite concealed. The disciples, who
must have brought him food, would surely
not have kept the secret. It would have become matter of conversation and rumour. In
truth, nothing was said against it, but in consequence of it great respect was shown, and
the religion spread far and wide. It cannot
be authoritatively denied that many saints have
visited the abodes of the angels, for the worlds
of heaven are beyond the knowledge of ordinary men."

Henceforward the book deals with none but
religious subjects. The first selections we
shall give are from his criticism of missionary
tracts, and his conversations with their writers.
Many readers will be shocked at his apparent
irreverence. We beg to remind such persons
that he, from education, sees these matters in
an utterly different light to what it is seen in

by believers in a God actively interested in the world, and also that he naturally feels justified in treating with ridicule the ideas of those foreigners who send to his country a body of missionaries, who spare little sarcasm or insult in their never-ceasing endeavours to bring his religion into contempt. He, as a Buddhist, might believe in the existence of a God sublimed above all human qualities and attributes, a perfect God, above love and hatred and jealousy, calmly resting in a quiet happiness that nothing could disturb, and of such a God he would speak no disparagement; not from desire to please him, or fear to offend him, but from natural veneration. But he cannot understand a God with the attributes and qualities of men, a God who loves and hates and shows anger, a Deity who, whether described to him by Christian Missionaries or by Mahometans, or Brahmins or Jews, falls below his standard of even an ordinary good man.

"I have studied the Roman Catholic book 'Maha Kangwon,' the Great Care, and it seems to me that the priests' great cares are their own interests. I see no attempt to explain any difficult and doubtful matters. If, as they say, God when he created man knew what every man would be, why did he create thieves? This is not explained. The book tells us that all those virtuous men who have taught religions differing from the Roman Catholic, have been enemies of God, but it does not explain why God has allowed so many different religions to arise and exist. How much do this and all other religions differ on this point from the religion of Buddha, which allows that there are eight kinds of holiness leading to ultimate happiness! (*i.e.* does not insist on Buddhism being necessary to salvation).

"The American missionary, Dr. Jones, wrote a book called the 'Golden Balance for weighing Buddhism and Christianity,' but I think any one who reads it will see that his balance is very one-sided; indeed, he who would weigh things ought to be able to look impartially at the scales.

"Dr. Gutzlaff declared that 'Somana Kodom only taught people to reverence himself and his disciples, saying, that by such means merit and heaven could be attained, teaching them

to respect the temples, and Po-trees, and everything in the temple grounds, lest by injuring
them they should go to hell, a teaching designed only for the protection of himself and
his disciples, and of no advantage to any
others.' I replied, 'In Christianity there is a
command to worship God alone, and no other ;
Mahomet also taught the worship of one only,
and promised that he would take into heaven
every one who joined his religion, even the
murderer of his parents, while those who would
not join his religion, however virtuous their
lives, should surely go to hell ; also he taught
that all other religions were the enemies of his
religion, and that heaven could be attained by
injuring the temples, idols, and anything
held sacred by another religion. Is such
teaching as that fit for belief? Buddha did
not teach that he alone should be venerated,
nor did he, the just one, ever teach that it was
right to persecute other religions. As for
adoration, so far as I know, men of every religion adore the holy one of their religion. It
is incorrect of the Doctor to say that Buddha taught men to adore him alone. He neither taught that such was necessary, nor

offered the alternative of hell as all other religions do.

"I said to the missionary, 'how about the
Dewas the Chinese believe in, are there any?'
He said 'No; no one has seen them; they do
not exist; there are only the angels, the servants of God, and the evil spirits whom God
drove out to be devils and deceive men.' I
said, 'Is there a God Jehovah?' He answered,
'Certainly, one God!' I rejoined, 'You said
there were no Dewas because no one had seen
them, why then do you assert the existence of
a God, for neither can we see him?' The
missionary answered, 'Truly, we see him not,
but all the works of creation must have a
master; they could not have originated of
themselves.' I said, 'There is no evidence of
the creation, it is only a tradition; why not
account for it by the self-producing power of
nature?' The missionary replied, 'that he had
no doubt but that God created everything, and
that not even a hair, or a grain of sand existed
of itself, for the things on the earth may be
likened to dishes of food arranged on a table,
and though no owner should be seen, none
would doubt but that there was one; no one

would think that the things came into the dishes of themselves.' I said, 'Then you consider that even a stone in the bladder is created by God!' He replied, 'Yes. Everything. God creates everything!' 'Then,' answered I, 'if that is so, God creates in man that which will cause his death, and you medical missionaries remove it and restore his health! Are you not opposing God in so doing? Are you not offending Him in curing those whom he would kill?' When I had said this the missionary became angry, and saying I was hard to teach, left me."

"Dr. Gutzlaff once said to me, 'Phra Somana Kodon, having entered Nippan, is entirely lost and non-existent, who, then, will give any return for recitations in his praise, benedictions, reverences, observances, and meritmaking? It is as a country without a king, where merit is unrewarded, because there is no one to reward it; but the religion of Jesus Christ has the Lord Jehovah and Christ to reward merit, and receive prayers and praises, and give a recompense.' I replied, 'It is true that, according to the Buddhist religion, the Lord Buddha does not give the reward of

merit; but if any do as he has taught, they
will find their recompense in the act. Even
when Buddha lived on earth, he had no power
to lead to heaven those who prayed for his
assistance, but did not honour and follow
the just way. The holy religion of Buddha is
perfect justice springing from a man's own
meritorious disposition. It is that disposition
which rewards the good and punishes the evil.
The recitations are the teachings of the Lord
Buddha, which are found in various Soodras,
set forms given by Buddha to holy hermits,
and some of them are descriptions of that which
is suitable and becoming in conduct. Even
though the Lord has entered Nippan, his grace
and benevolence are not exhausted. You missionaries praise the grace of Jehovah and
Christ, and say that the Lord waits to hear
and grant the prayers of those that call to
Him. But are those prayers granted? So
far as I see, they get no more than people
who do not believe in prayer. They die the
same, and they are equally liable to age and
disease and sorrow. How, then, can you say
that your religion is better than any other?
In the Bible we find that God created Adam

and Eve, and desired that they should have no
sickness nor sorrow, nor know death; but because they, the progenitors of mankind, ate of
a forbidden fruit, God became angry, and or-
dained that thenceforth they should endure
toil and weariness, and trouble and sickness,
and from that time fatigue and sorrow, and
. sickness and death fell upon mankind. It
was said that by baptism men should be free
from the curse of Adam, but I do not see that
any one who is baptized now-a-days is free
from the curse of Adam, or escapes toil and
grief, and sickness and death, any more than
those who are not baptized.' The missionary
answered, 'Baptism for the remission of sin
is only effectual in gaining heaven after death,
for those who die unbaptized will certainly go
to hell.' But the Missionary did not explain
the declaration that by baptism men should be
free from pains and troubles in their present
state. He further said, 'It does at times please
God to accede to the requests of those that
pray to Him, a remarkable instance of which
is, that Europeans and Americans have more
excellent arts than any other people. Have
they not steamboats and railways, and tele-

graphs and manufactures, and guns and weapons of war superior to any others in the world? Are not the nations which do not worship Christ comparatively ignorant?' I asked the Doctor about sorrow and sickness, things which prevail throughout the world, things in which Christians have no advantage over other men, but he would not reply on that point, and spoke only of matters of knowledge. Where is the witness who can say that this knowledge was the gift of God? There are many in Europe who do not believe in God, but are indifferent, yet have subtle and expanded intellects, and are great philosophers and politicians. How is it that God grants to these men, who do not believe in Him, the same intelligence He grants to those who do? Again, how is it that the Siamese, Burmese, Cochin Chinese, and other Roman Catholic converts, whom we see more attentive to their religion than the Europeans who reside among us, do not receive some reward for their merit, and have superior advantages and intelligence to those who are not converted. So far as I can see, the reverse is the case: the unconverted flourish, but the con-

verted are continually in debt and bondage.
There are many converts in Siam, but I see
none of them rise to wealth, so as to become
talked about. They continually pray to God,
but, it seems, nothing happens according to
their prayer.' The missionary replied, ' They
are Roman Catholics, and hold an untrue religion, therefore God is not pleased with them.'
I said to the missionary, ' You say that God
sometimes grants the prayers of those who
pray to Him ; now, the Chinese, who pray to
spirits and devils, sometimes obtain what they
have prayed for ; do you not, therefore, allow
that these spirits can benefit man ?' The missionary answered, ' The devil receives bribes.'
I inquired, ' Among the men and animals God
creates, some die in the womb, and many at
or immediately after birth, and before reaching maturity, and many are deaf, dumb. and
crippled : why are such created ? Is it not a
waste of labour ? Again, God creates men,
and does not set their hearts to hold to His
religion, but sets them free to take false religions, so that they are all damned, while those
who worship Him go to heaven : is not this in-
consistent with His goodness and mercy ? If

He, indeed, created all men, would He not have shown equal compassion and goodness to all, and not allowed inequalities? Then I should have believed in a creating God. But, as it is, it seems nothing but a game at dolls.' The missionary replied, ' With regard to long and short lives, the good may live but a short time, God being pleased to call them to heaven, and sometimes He permits the wicked to live to a full age, that they may repent of their sins. And the death of innocent children is the mercy of God calling them to heaven.' I rejoined, ' How should God take a special liking to unlovable, shapeless, unborn children?' The missionary replied, ' He who would learn to swim must practise in shallow places first, or he will be drowned. If any spoke like this in European countries, he would be put in prison.' I invite particular attention to this statement.

"Another time I said to the missionary Gutzlaff, ' It is said in the Bible that God is the creator of all men and animals. Why should he not create them spontaneously, as worms and vermin arise from filth, and fish are formed in new pools by the emanations of

air and water? Why must there be procreation, and agony and often death to mothers?
Is not this labour lost? I can see no good in
it.' He replied, 'God instituted procreation
so that men might know their fathers and
mothers and relatives, and the pains of child-
birth are a consequence of the curse of Adam.'
I said, ' If procreation was designed that men
should know their relatives, why are animals,
which do not know their relatives, produced
in the same manner? And why do they, not
being descendants of Eve, suffer pain in labour
for her sin of eating a little forbidden fruit?
Besides, the Bible says, by belief in Christ man
shall escape the consequences of Eve's sin, yet I
cannot see that men do so escape in any degree,
but suffer just as others do.' The missionary
answered, ' It is waste of time to converse with
evil men who will not be taught,' and so left me.

"The Lord Buddha declined to discourse on
the creation; he said that there was no beginning, and that the subject was unprofitable, as
such knowledge was no help towards diminish-
ing misery. I doubt not that he knew the
truth, and would not tell it, because it would
have shocked the prejudices of his hearers,

Brahmins who believed that various classes of men had sprung from different parts of the Creator's body, and who had instituted caste according to the more or less honourable part of the body from which they thought that certain classes had sprung. Those who believe in God the Creator tell us that the creation occupied six days, the sun, moon, and stars being created on the fourth. Now the number of stars is infinite, and each star or sun is greater than the earth by as much as a fortress is greater than a pea. How can we believe that God made this inconceivable infinity of immense things in one day, and yet required five days to make this little world, this mere drop in the great ocean?

"I asked the Mussulmans and missionaries, 'if God created all things, and is ruler of the world, and has spirit and knowledge, and judgment to reward the good and punish the wicked, what merit did he make in former times that he should become the Great God of Heaven?' They answered, 'not by acquired merit, but by himself did God exist. As in numbers you have two, and three, and four upwards, but they all depend on the first, or one, and none can say whence comes one.' I asked, ' The elements of the world are endless, space is infinite, men and animals infinite, the worlds in space uncountable; if the spirit of God is single, how can it fill them all and search out everything in the disposition of men, and watch the good and evil in every heart?' They replied, ' the power of God is great, wherever there is space, God is.' "

Nearly fifty pages of the ' Kitchanukit' are taken up by the sketch of the religions of the world.

" There are philosophers who say that all known sects may be classed under two religions only, the Brahmanyang and the Samanyang. All those who pray for assistance to Brahma, Indra, God the Creator, Angels, Devils, Parents, or other intercessors or possible benefactors,—all who believe in the existence of any being who can help them, and in the efficacy of prayer, are Brahmanyang; while all who believe that they must depend solely on the inevitable results of their own acts, that good and evil are consequences of preceding causes, and that merit and demerit are the regulators of existence, and who therefore do not pray to any to help them, and all those who profess to know nothing of what will happen after death, and all those who disbelieve in a future existence, are Samanyang.

"Brahminism is," he writes, "the most ancient known religion, held by numbers of men to this day, though with many varieties of belief. Its fundamental doctrine was that the world was created by Tao Maha Phrom (Brahma), who divided his nature into two parts, Isuen (Vishnu), Lord of the Earth and rewarder of the good, and Narai (Siva), Lord of the Ocean, and punisher of the wicked. The Brahmins believed in blood sacrifices, which they offered before idols with three faces and six hands, representing three gods in one. Sometimes they made separate images of the three, and called them the father, the son, and the spirit, all three being one, and the son being that part of the deity which at various times is born in the earth as a man, the Avatar of God.

After Brahminism he treats of Judaism.

"About 3000 years ago a Kёk,* named Abra-

---

* This word is applied to Jews and Mahometans, whatever country they are natives of.

ham, who lived in Koran (? Chaldæa), the son
of a Brahmin priest, dreamt that the Lord Allah
came and told him that it was not right to worship images, and that he must destroy his idols
and flee from that country, and establish a new
religion, permitting no kneeling or sacrifice
except to God alone. Animal sacrifice was to
be retained, and the followers of his religion
were to be circumcised instead of being baptized. For without circumcision none is a fol-
lower of Islam."

He continues with the story of Abraham and
his trial, as told in the Bible, ending with the
remark : " Thus the religion of Islam branched
off from Brahminism." Next follows a short
account of the separation of Christianity from
Judaism, and the introduction of the rite of
baptism, of which he observes :—

" Baptism was a religious rite from very ancient times, the Brahmins holding that if any
one who had sinned went to the bank of the
Ganges, and saying ' I will not sin again,'
plunged into the stream, he would rise to the
surface free of sin, all his sins floating away
with the water. Hence it was called baptism,
or the rite of washing off offences so that they

floated away. Sometimes when any one was sick
unto death, his relatives would place him by the
river, and give him water to drink, and pour
water over him till he died, believing that he
would thus die holy and go to heaven. This
was the old belief, the rite of circumcision
being introduced by the prophet Abraham, and
it is to be supposed that the holy man John
(the Baptist) thought that the ancient rite
was the proper one, and so restored it."

Next follows an account of the second great
offspring of the religion of Abraham, Mahometanism, the rise of which and its division
into two sects, Soonnees and Mahous (Sheres),
are treated of at some length. This religion,
he observes, was not spread by the arguments
of preachers, but by men who held the Koran
with one hand and the sword with the other.
We will not occupy our reader's time by quot-
ing the history of Mahometanism, which they
can read elsewhere, but they may be amused
by the account of the reason that pork is forbidden food.

"They say that when men first filled the
world, Allah forbade them to eat any animals
but such as died a natural death; and as the

animals would not die as quickly as they wished,
they accelerated their deaths by striking them
and throwing things at them. The animals
complained to Allah of this treatment, and he
sent his angel Gabriel to order all men and
animals to assemble together that he might decide the case. But the pigs were disobedient
and did not come. Then Allah said, ' The pigs,
the lowest of animals, are disobedient, let no
one eat them or touch them.' "

His remarks on other religions we quote in
his own words :—

" Another religion is what the Siamese call
that of the Lord Phoot (Phra Phutthi Chao),
and Europeans call that of Somana Kodour or
Gautama, or Buddha. Its followers, some of
them, walk reverently according to the rules
called Thamwinai, others follow a relaxed code.
In some countries the monks are treated as
kings. Christianity is also a great religion.
Christians were originally all Roman Catholics.
The Roman Catholics believed in Jehovah and
Christ and Mary, the mother, and in saints and
in the Pope, the great bishop of Rome, who
they say is the substitute for Christ on earth
with power to absolve from sin, and to order

doctrines. The priests of that religion, whom we call Bat Huang, dress in black and have no wives. After many centuries certain Germans considered that the Roman Catholic tenets were contrary to the Bible, so they formed a new sect, believing in God and Christ only. Their teachers are called missionaries, and dress like ordinary people and have wives, and if their wives die can marry again, though some hold that they should not do so. They do not worship Mary, the mother, nor the saints; many left the old religion to join this sect. Another sect are the Mormons; they say that their religion arose from certain men dreaming that God in heaven took a golden plate whereon was written the holy doctrine, and buried it in the earth. And those who dreamt thus dug, and found a scripture engraven on a plate of gold, according to their dream. Then they believed in God in heaven, and Christ and polygamy, and doing as they pleased; the rules of their religion being much more lax than those of Roman Catholics or Christians (Protestants). And they believed that if they turned their thoughts to Christ when at the point of death, Christ would take their souls to heaven. All

these three sects worship the same God and
Christ, why then should they blame each other,
and charge each other with believing wrongly,
and say to each other, ' you are wrong and will
go to hell, we are right and shall go to heaven' ?
It is one religion, yet how can we join it when
each party threatens us with hell if we agree
with the other, and there is none to decide between them. I beg comparison of this with
the teaching of the Lord Buddha, that who-
ever endeavours to keep the Commandments,*
and is charitable, and walks virtuously must
attain to heaven." A few remarks on the worship
of Juggernauth, fire-worship, Confucianism,
spirit-worship, and unbelief, and a sketch of
the principal localities of each religion conclude this subject.

The next question is, out of so many religions, how shall a man select that which he
can trust to for his future happiness ?

" He must reflect, and apply his mind to
ascertain which is most true. This is a subject of constant dispute, every one upholding
his own religion. Even the lowest of man-

* For an account of the five Commandments, see
page 72.

kind, devil worshippers, have faith in their own belief, and will not hear those who would teach them differently. It is very hard for men to relinquish their first ideas and habits. Those who do change their religions are either poor people who do it out of respect to those who have helped them when in difficulties, or those who have been persecuted and forced to change, or those who are induced, by observing the superior skill and knowledge of the followers of any religion, to believe that their religion must be the true one; or those who change their religion for that of some one whom they respect as much wiser and better than themselves, and sure to be right in everything, or those who do it to get help when they have lawsuits, and to obtain protectors against oppression. Also there are those who, having listened to teaching, are enlightened, and see clearly that form and name are not realities, and must be considered as sorrows, and that there is no help to be had from any one, but that good and evil are the result of merit and demerit. Some there are who have become Buddhists on these considerations."

On this subject he quotes one of the Soodras, supposed to be a sermon of Buddha :—

" There is a Buddhist Soodra which pleased
me much when I read it, and I have remem-
bered it, and will repeat it here, begging to
be excused for variations, omissions, and ad-
ditions, as it is intended for those who are
not learned in the holy religion of Buddha.
It is as follows: On a certain occasion the
Lord Buddha led a number of his disciples to
a village of the Kalamachon, where his wisdom
and merit and holiness were known. And
the Kalamachon assembled, and did homage
to him, and said, ' Many priests and Brahmins
have at different times visited us, and explained their religious tenets, declaring them
to be excellent, but each abused the tenets of
every one else, whereupon we are in doubt as
to whose religion is right and whose wrong;
but we have heard that the Lord Buddha
teaches an excellent religion, and we beg that
we may be freed from doubt, and learn the
truth.'

" And the Lord Buddha answered, ' You
were right to doubt, for it was a doubtful
matter. I say unto all of you, Do not believe in what ye have heard; that is, when you
have heard any one say this is especially good

or extremely bad; do not reason with yourselves that if it had not been true, it would
not have been asserted, and so believe in its
truth. Neither have faith in traditions, because they have been handed down for many
generations and in many places.

" ' Do not believe in anything because it is
rumoured and spoken of by many; do not think
that it is a proof of its truth.

" ' Do not believe merely because the written
statement of some old sage is produced; do
not be sure that the writing has ever been re-
vised by the said sage, or can be relied on.
Do not believe in what you have fancied,
thinking that because an idea is extraordinary,
it must have been implanted by a Dewa, or
some wonderful being.

" ' Do not believe in guesses, that is, assum-
ing something at hap-hazard as a starting-point
draw your conclusions from it; reckoning your
two and your three and your four before you
have fixed your number one.

" ' Do not believe because you think there
is analogy, that is a suitability in things and
occurrences, such as believing that there must
be walls of the world, because you see water

in a basin; or that Mount Meru must exist, because you have seen the reflection of trees; or that there must be a creating God, because houses and towns have builders.

"'Do not believe in the truth of that to which you have become attached by habit, as every nation believes in the superiority of its own dress and ornaments and language.

"'Do not believe because your informant appears to be a credible person, as, for instance, when you see any one having a very sharp appearance, conclude that he must be clever and trustworthy; or when you see any one who has powers and abilities beyond what men generally possess, believe in what he tells. Or think that a great nobleman is to be believed, as he would not be raised by the king to high station unless he were a good man.

"'Do not believe merely on the authority of your teachers and masters, or believe and practise merely because they believe and practise.

"'I tell you all, you must of your own selves know that "this is evil, this is punishable, this is censured by wise men, belief in this will bring no advantage to one, but will cause sorrow." And when you know this, then eschew it.

" ' I say to all of you dwellers in Kalamachon, answer me this. Lopho, that is covetousness, Toso, that is anger and savageness, and Moho, that is ignorance and folly,—when any or all of these arise in the hearts of men, is the result beneficial or the reverse ?'

" And they answered, ' It is not beneficial, O Lord.'

" Then the Lord continued, ' Covetous, passionate, and ignorant men destroy life and steal, and commit adultery and tell lies, and incite others to follow their example, is it not so ?'

" And they answered, ' It is as the Lord says.'

" And he continued, ' Covetousness, passion, ignorance, the destruction of life, theft, adultery, and lying, are these good or bad, right or wrong ? do wise men praise or blame them ? Are they not unprofitable, and causes of sorrow ?'

" And they replied, ' It is as the Lord has spoken.'

" And the Lord said, ' For this I said to you, do not believe merely because you have heard, but when of your own consciousness you know a thing to be evil, abstain from it.'

"And then the Lord taught of that which is good, saying, 'If any of you know of yourselves that anything is good and not evil, praised by wise men, advantageous, and productive of happiness, then act abundantly according to your belief. Now I ask you, Alopho, absence of covetousness, Atoso, absence of passion, Amoho, absence of folly, are these profitable or not?'

"And they answered, 'Profitable.'

"The Lord continued, 'Men who are not covetous, or passionate, or foolish will not destroy life, nor steal, nor commit adultery nor tell lies, is it not so?'

"And they answered, 'It is as the Lord says.'

"Then the Lord asked, 'Is freedom from covetousness, passion, and folly, from destruction of life, theft, adultery, and lying, good or bad, right or wrong, praised or blamed by wise men, profitable and tending to happiness or not?'

"And they replied, 'It is good, right, praised by the wise, profitable, and tending to happiness.'

"And the Lord said, 'For this I taught you not to believe merely because you have heard,

but when you believed of your own consciousness, then to act accordingly and abundantly.'

"And the Lord continued, 'The holy man
must not be covetous or revengeful or foolish,
and he must be versed in the four Phromma-
wihan, which are, Pemetta, desiring for all
living things the same happiness which one
seeks for oneself; Karuna, training the mind
in compassion towards all living things, desiring that they may escape all sorrows either in
hell or in other existences, just as a man who
sees his friend ill, desires nothing so much as
his recovery; Muthita, taking pleasure in all
living things, just as playmates are glad when
they see one another; and Ubekkha, keeping
the mind balanced and impartial, with no affection for one more than another.' "

From another Soodra we extract the following passage :—

"Consider! Can you respect or believe in
religions which recommend actions that bring
happiness to oneself by causing sorrow to
others, or happiness to others by sorrow to
oneself, or sorrow to both oneself and others?

"Is not that a better religion which pro-
motes the happiness of others simultaneously

with the happiness of oneself, and tolerates no oppression?"

The next subject we deal with is the future state :—

"Some men believe that merit and demerit cause successive rebirths of the soul until it becomes perfect, when it is not born again. Others believe that after death the soul is next born in heaven or hell, and has no further change. Others believe that man is reborn as man, and every animal born again in its kind for ever. Others believe that there is no resurrection of the dead. I have pondered much on this subject, and cannot absolutely decide it. If we were to believe that death is annihilation, we should be at a loss to account for the existence of mankind.

"If we were to hold with those who believe in God the Creator, it should follow that (the impartial justice of God) would make all men and animals equal in life and similar in nature, which is not the case. But if we believe in the interchange and succession of life throughout all beings (i.e. the transmigration of souls), and that good and evil arise from ourselves, and are the effects of merit and demerit, we

have some grounds for belief. The differences
of men and animals afford a very striking proof,
clear to our eyes."

The argument here is, that as some men and
animals have a superior lot to others, there
must needs follow other successive states to
compensate those whose present condition is
inferior, unless we suppose the difference of
present condition to be caused by the merits
and demerits of a previous existence. Either
supposition, he considers, affords proof of his
proposition, and requires only one presump-
tion, viz. that the law of the world is perfect
justice:—

"Those who believe that after death the
soul passes to hell or heaven for ever, have no
proof that there is no return thence. Certainly,
it would be a most excellent thing to go direct
to heaven after death, without further change,
but I am afraid that it is not the case. For
the believers in it, who have not perfectly
purified their hearts and prepared themselves
for that most excellent place where there is no
being born, growing old, and dying, will still
have their souls contaminated with uneradi-
cated evil, the fruit of evil deeds, for where
else can that evil go to?

"That there is a place of perfect happiness, where there is no being born or growing old or dying, was known only to him who attained the perfection of holiness. He said that there is really such a place, but none of us have seen it, and we know not the condition of the Lord Buddha's soul.

"The worker in gold cannot make anything of his gold until he has refined it from all impurities. Subsequent meltings will not then affect it, because it is pure. In like manner the Lord before he ceased to breathe had repressed and cleared away all evil from his soul, so that it could not return, and there remained nothing but good. Being pure we can conceive that, like the pure gold, it might pass to where it would be affected by no further change. How is it possible that those who have not cleared away the evil disposition from their soul should attain the most excellent heaven, and live eternally with God the Creator? and of those who are to remain in hell for ever, many have made merit, and done much good. Shall that be altogether lost?

"The Lord Buddha taught, saying, 'All you who are in doubt as to whether or not there is

a future life, had better believe that there is
one, that there is another existence, in which
happiness and misery can be felt.   It is better
to believe this than otherwise, for if the heart
believes in a future life it will abandon sin and
act virtuously ; and even if there is no resurrection, such a life will bring a good name and
the regard of men.   But those who believe in
extinction at death will not fail to commit any
sin that they may choose because of their dis-
belief in a future ; and if there should happen
to be a future after all, they will be at a disad-
vantage, they will be like travellers without
provisions.'

"Buddha seeing the doubt in some men's
minds, as to birth and extinction, was pleased
to preach thus."

This argument is followed by stories from
the sacred books illustrating transmigration,
and by several anecdotes of the present time
of children who, as soon as they could speak,
have asserted and given proofs of their having
previously existed as men or animals; one
example is enough.

"Another instance is that of the child of
a Peguan, at Paklat (a town near Bangkok),

who, as soon as he had learned to speak, told his parents that he was formerly named Makran, and had been killed by a fall from a cocoanut-tree, and that as he fell his hatchet fell from his hand and dropped into a ditch. And they seeing that his story coincided with something that had happened within their knowledge, tried the child by making him point out the tree, and he pointed out the tree, and his story was confirmed by their digging up the hatchet from the ditch."

The next question is, what is it that is re-born?

"It is difficult to explain whether it is the same or another life which is born again in a future state. It may be compared to the seeds of plants which sprout and grow and produce more seed, can the succeeding tree and seed be said to be the same as the original tree and seed? So it is in this case. To dwell on the subject would be tedious. Again, is the echo the same sound as that to which it answers, or another sound? The condition in which the new birth will take place must be dependent on the necessity which the being has itself caused by the state of its disposition, for merit and demerit are the orderers of the place of the new birth and the preparers of increasing happiness or misery."

We are next told that all entry into a new state is effected in one of four ways, i.e., by production in the egg, by ordinary birth, by life resulting from emanations of earth and water and change of leaves, etc., as vermin result from filth, fish from emanations in new pools, insects from fruits, and snakes from a certain vine; and fourthly by spontaneous appearance without birth, as angels and devils originate.

The subject of a future life will be again reverted to after our readers have had set before them the nature of the directing influence of merit and demerit, of that law of nature or guiding power with which Buddhists supply the place of God. The Siamese call this Kam, and it is sometimes translated as fate or consequence. We shall use the word kam in preference to any translation.

We may aid our readers to comprehend this Kam by giving a short account of its action before proceeding further with quotations.

Buddhists believe that every act, word, or

thought has its consequence, which will appear sooner or later in the present or in some future state. Evil acts will produce evil consequences, that is may cause a man misfortune in this· world, or an evil birth in hell, or as an animal in some future existence. Good acts, etc., will produce good consequences; prosperity in this world, or birth in heaven, or in a high position in the world in some future state. When we say every act, etc., has its effect, we must make the exception that where several acts, etc., are of such a nature that their result will be the same in kind, and due at the same time, then only one of the said acts, etc., will produce an effect, and the others will be neutralized, or become "Ahosikam." Sometimes even single acts may become effectless or "Ahosikam," as will be explained further on.

There is no God who judges of these acts, etc., and awards recompense or punishment, but the reward or punishment is simply the inevitable effect of Kam which works out its own results.

Our author quotes from the 'Attha Katha Chari' and 'Atthanomati,' ancient and canonical commentaries, interposing with much deference a few explanations of his own :—

"The meritorious and demeritorious Kam, which living beings have caused to exist by their own acts, words, or thoughts, are, whether their fruits be joy or sorrow, to be classed under three heads.

"The first is Tittham Wetaniya Kam, that is the Kam of which creatures will have the fruits at once, in their present state of existence.

"The second is Upacha Wetaniya Kam, that is the Kam of which creatures will have the fruits in the next state of existence.

"The third is Oprapara Wetaniya Kam, that is the Kam of which creatures will have the fruits in future states of existence from the third onward.

"Merit or demerit will cause a tendency of the soul in one direction sometimes to as many as seven births and deaths, which will be followed by a relapse in the opposite direction for six, five, or less times; such is the way of the soul.

"The merit of a single act of charity, or the demerit of the slaughter of a single ant, will be certainly followed by one of these three Kams.

Then followed anecdotes of Tittham Wetaniya Kam, telling how men have been rewarded for a distinguished act of goodness by a sudden change from poverty to wealth; and how for an act of cruelty horrible sufferings have been almost instantaneously experienced.

"Merit or demerit of this class must have their fruit in the present existence. If they do not they will become 'Ahosikam,' lost altogether. They will be like a bowshot which misses the animal it is aimed at, or like fruit which a man has gathered and forgotten to eat until it has turned rotten.

"Meritorious Upacha Wetaniya Kam, of which the fruits appear in the next existence (that following the one in which the works which caused it were done), is produced by the eight states of pious meditation (Samabatti), and will assuredly cause rebirth in the superior heavens; but as any one of the eight would of itself be followed by this Kam, and cause the same heavenly birth, and as the effect is one which can happen in the second and no other existence, it follows that he who has attained all the eight Samabatti will but receive the result of one, and the other seven will be lost or Ahosikam.

"Demeritorious Upacha Wetaniya Kam is caused by parricide, matricide, killing saints, defiling Buddha with blood,* and dispersing monks. Any one of these will cause rebirth in hell, and the commission of more than one of these sins will make no difference. The others will be lost or Ahosikam, for they have no power in any other existence.

"Oprapara Wetaniya Kam differs from the preceding, in that it can never be lost or Ahosikam. Every act of which the Kam is of this class, whether meritorious or demeritorious, will certainly have its fruits in some generation, from the third onward, whenever the suitable time may come.

"The 'Atthanomati' states, 'This present existence, from the time that Kam is incurred until death, is the domain of Tittham Wetaniya Kam ; when it has power, it produces its effects within this limit; when it has not enough power to produce its effects within this limit, its domain is ended by death, and it becomes Ahosikam. The whole of the second exist-

---

* Our author remarks that as Buddha has passed to Nippan, and there are now no saints, it is no longer possible to commit these two sins.

ence is the domain of Upacha Wetaniya Kam ;
when it has power enough, it gives its fruits
within that time, but when it has not power
enough to do so, it becomes Ahosikam. From
the time of entering on the third existence
and onwards, is the domain of Oprapara Wetaniya Kam, which ends only with the attainment of Nippan, the cessation from further
change.' "

Kam is again divided under four heads—
Kru, Pahula, Asanna, and Kotta—according to
the time when its effects will appear, which
depends on comparative importance. The more
important the act, the sooner will the effect
come. First of Kru Kam :—

"The most powerful of all demeritorious
Kam is the result of the five before-mentioned
sins (parricide, etc.) ; when any one of these
has been committed, not even a hundred years
of merit-making will secure happiness, or prevent the soul going to hell at death. The
most powerful meritorious Kam results from
the eight states of Samabatti (pious meditation)."

We omit, as of less interest, the remarks on
Pahula and Asanna Kam ; the first, meaning

Kam which is important from its nature, the second, Kam which is rendered important by the circumstances of the action giving rise to it, as a good or bad act done at the point of death; and we quote the account of Kotta Kam, the lightest Kam :—

"Kotta Kam is light, small, not made at the point of death, and made in ignorance of its being meritorious or demeritorious. As, for instance, when men, not knowing that they are doing a meritorious act, remove a stake or thorn, or tile from the road, lest it may hurt any one passing along, or, seeing any kind of filth, lying in a public place, remove it, and cleanse the place; or where a child, seeing its parents make offerings and bow to a Prachedi,* imitates them, this is meritorious Kotta Kam.

"Demeritorious Kotta Kam arises when men, not knowing that they are doing wrong, kill or strike small animals, regarding them as vegetables; and when children playfully do mischievous tricks, and when any wrong is com-

* Prachedi are spires in temples, generally covering a relic or image of Buddha, and supposed to lead the thoughts to the teachings of the Great Teacher.

mitted in ignorance. In the absence of other Kam, this Kam will operate at some stage of existence, causing happiness or sorrow, according as it is meritorious or demeritorious."

The afore mentioned divisions of Kam, under three heads and four heads, refer to time and gravity; it is also divided into four classes according to the nature of its action. They are Chanaka aKm, Upatampaka Kam, Upa-pilaka Kam, and Upakhathaka Kam. The first is the Kam which causes birth or existence in any particular state of happiness or sorrow; the second modifies that state by causing its prolongation; the third modifies it by reducing the amount of happiness or misery; and the last violently opposes itself to any existing Kam, so as to destroy its effects. This last Kam is illustrated by the story of 'Augkuliman.'

"Augkuliman, whilst yet a layman, committed nine hundred and ninety-nine murders, but afterwards, by attaining to saintly perfection, he obtained an Upakhathaka Kam, which cut off the Kam of the murders he had committed. He acquired meritorious Upacha Wetaniya Kam, of which he would enjoy the fruits in his next generation, and meritorious Opra-

para Wetaniya Kam, of which he would enjoy
the fruits in the third and subsequent generations. There was left only Tittham Wetaniya Kam, by which his murders could have
any effect; and it did have effect, causing him,
after he had attained his saintly condition, to
be accidently pelted with sticks and lumps of
earth."

Such are the eleven Kam of the Attha Katha
Chari, the last eight being only the same as
the first three, but differently described. Next
follows a passage comparing the idea of Kam
with that of a divine judge.

" These Kam we have discoursed about have
no substance, and we cannot see where they
exist, nor when they are about to have effect
do they come crying, ' I am the Kam, named
So-and-so, come to give fruits to such a
one.' This I have only adverted to for comparison, with the belief of some that there is
a creating God who causes existences. Those
who so believe cannot see the Creator better
than others see the Kam. It is a matter for
the consideration of the wise, whether we
should say there is a creating God, the Lord
and Master of the world, or should say that it

is Kam which fashions and causes existences. Neither has a visible form. If we believe that Kam is the cause, the creator, the arranger, we can get hold of the end of the thread, and understand that the happiness and misery of living beings is all caused by natural sequence. But if we assert that a creating God is the dispenser of happiness and misery, we must believe that He is everywhere, and at all times watching and trying, and deciding what punishments are due to the countless multitude of men. Is this credible? Moreover, we are told that the Creator made animals to be food for man; these animals enjoy happiness and suffer misery, like as human beings do. How, can we then say that the Creator does not grant them justice, and give them also a future state of reward and punishment?

From this disquisition on Kam, we pass to the duties of a good Buddhist. The question is put, "If a man believes in a future existence governed by Kam, how shall he make merit to save himself from future misery?" The answer to this is of course, "By following the teachings of Buddha, the holy and omniscient, the teaching which praises kindness, and compassion, and pleasure in the general happiness of all beings, and freedom from love or dislike to individuals, and which forbids hatred and jealousy, and envy and revenge; the religion which teaches Than, or almsgiving, and Sin, or rules of morality." Than, or almsgiving, is explained as follows:—

"Than is the voluntary gift of anything not injurious. If there is no intention to give, or the gift is harmful (as poison or spirits), it is not Than. Furthermore, there must be either the desire to assist, or the desire to show gratitude.

"The desire to assist is manifested when a layman gives foods to monks, reflecting that monks must starve unless laymen feed them; also when a man, from compassionate motives, gives anything to a beggar; and also in a lower degree when a man gives food to animals merely from the knowledge that without his assistance they would die.

"The desire to show gratitude is manifested in gifts to parents, and others entitled to respectful regard, especially to holy and distinguished men.

"It is not Than when gifts are given from

other considerations, as when animals are fed that they may be used, or presents are given by lovers to bind affection, or given to slaves to stimulate labour.

"Sages and religious men have observed that Than is an universal merit, existing at all times and in all countries. It was a practice of old, it is a practice now, and it will be a practice in future in all countries and among all people, sometimes more, sometimes less, sometimes having much fruit, and sometimes not being genuine and having but little fruit. I now beg to speak of it as practised at the present day, and to point out what is praiseworthy, and what censurable, according to my own observation. The following descriptions of almsgiving are very meritorious :—

"Firstly, when a man reflecting that his present wealth is but the result of causation in previous existences, and that it is his duty to make merit for future existences, and not hoard up that which is unstable; and that so long as there are wearers of the yellow robe, the religion will exist, but that if none assist them the monks must die out,—eagerly devises means to promote the religion of Buddha, and

ensure its permanence, and with that view
erects temples, monasteries, spires, and preach-
ing-houses where religious exercises may be
practised, and the monks may cherish their
religion in peace, and be a leaven for the future.
This is most excellent almsgiving.

"Another kind is when a man seeks the
happiness and pleasure of all men, those he
loves and those he hates, those he has a cause
of revenge against, and those against whom he
has none, and with that view digs canals and
pools, and makes roads and bridges and salas,
and plants large trees to give shade.   This
generally diffused charity is most excellent
almsgiving.

"Another is, when any show kindness to
their elder relatives, parents, etc., seeking their
happiness during their lives, and showing
respect by merit-making and almsgiving after
their deaths.   This, too, is very meritorious.

"Another is, when from compassion to the
poor and miserable who have none to help
them, and suffer extreme misery, a man erects
rest-houses and drinking-fountains, and gives
them food and clothes, and necessaries and
medicine for their ailments, without selecting

one more than another. This is true charity, and has much fruit.

"There are four classes who make merit by almsgiving without pure compassion and piety. One class does it for show, another from greediness, another from jealousy, and another from envy.

"Those who do it for show are such as without any real desire to aid religion, or genuine feeling of compassion, make merit as they see others do, from a desire to display their wealth, not for future advantage. Sometimes they do not even own the gifts they pretend to bestow, and hire them for half-a-crown from some priest who owns them, and give him another half-crown to carry them away, ostentatiously piled up on a stand.

"Those who do it from greediness are such as having much wealth distribute it before their death, partly to prevent their heir getting it, and partly in hopes that they will be rewarded by going to heaven, and having tens of thousands of houris to minister to them.

"Another class makes merit from jealousy; as when some person of property dies, and the administrator of his estate, in order to prevent some person receiving a share, distributes the whole in alms and merit-making.*

"Another class gives alms from envy, that is, when they see an enemy make merit in any way, they go and make more merit, not from piety, but from a desire to be born in their next existence in a superior condition to that their enemy will have.

"Let no one who makes merit by giving alms have such a disposition as any of these."

Ostentatious merit-making is common among all the Siamese. The kings annually, in person or by deputy, make offerings at the principal temples throughout the country, accompanied by procession of sometimes more than a hundred state barges, bands of music, and every material of display. Those who can afford it combine in similar processions on a smaller scale; even poor people will, from time to time, invite two or three monks to receive some trumpery presents at their houses, and will proclaim the fact by beating a drum for several hours. The Siamese certainly sup-

* It does sometimes happen that all the estate of the deceased is expended in a great entertainment and feast given at the cremation of the body.

port their priests well, not only by occasional gifts of clothing, etc. but by daily gifts of food.

Much money is also spent in the other ways designated by our author, the construction of temples especially. He himself is now, and has been for years, superintending the building of one called Pratom Prachidee, near Bangkok, which will, when finished, be one of the finest and largest Buddhist temples in the world. It is built principally with funds supplied by the late king, who also built many other temples. It is unfortunate that the desire is always to build new temples rather than to repair old ones, so that there are but too many temples in a ruinous condition.

Charity of the kind which is best known in England is scarcely ever called for in Siam, where it is easy to live with but little labour, and where the respect shown to family ties and the prevalence of a mild system of slavery enable almost every one to support himself, or get supported without recourse to beggary.

It is only just to the Siamese to add, that though fond of ostentatious almsgiving, as above said, they are also privately charitable, and kind and hospitable to strangers.

From "Than" we pass to "Sin," which means "abstinence" from breaking the Five Commandments, but is as often used for the Commandments themselves. The Five Commandments are:—

1st. Thou shalt not destroy, nor cause the destruction of any living thing.

2nd. Thou shalt not, either by fraud or violence, obtain or keep that which belongs to another.

3rd. Thou shalt not lie carnally with any but proper objects for thy lust.

4th. Thou shalt not attempt, either by word or action, to lead others to believe that which is not true.

5th. Thou shalt not become intoxicated.

The offence of breaking these Commandments may be greater or less according to the quality of the person injured by the act, the amount of premeditation leading to the act, the desire or passion which causes the act, and lastly, the object of the act, *i.e.* the value of the thing stolen, the damage done by a lie, etc. We give one example of the way in which these commandments are analysed.

"There are five essentials of Athinnathan

(the 2nd Commandment). 1st. Property which
another sets store by. 2nd. Knowledge that
it is so. 3rd. Intention to get possession of it.
4th. Means taken to do so personally or by
agent. 5th. Obtaining said property against
the owner's will."

In the same manner, for a breach of the
other Commandments, there must be not only
a completed act, but also intention.

Excellent as these Commandments are, few
men keep them all.

"At the present time very few men, even
Buddhists, perfectly observe these five Commandments. Some can abstain from all but
lying. Others take care not to destroy large
animals, but cannot restrain themselves from
killing gad-flies and mosquitoes. Some can
keep from actual theft, but not from getting
other people's property by oppression and
fraud. Some can refrain from other men's
wives, but not from their daughters. Some
can keep from great lies, such as bearing false
witness, but will tell other lies, such as saying
they have not seen or heard, when they have
seen or heard, regarding these as trifling
offences. As for drunkenness, some abstain

from all intoxicating things even in medicine, others take them in moderation.

"He who cannot abstain from these five offences is guilty—not because the religion of Buddha is cruel, and forbids that which men best like and cannot abstain from, or because the rules are cruel and will cause misfortune to those who believe in them—but because of his own passions.

"The observance of these Five Commandments is good at all times, and in all places. There has never been and there never will be a wise man who would not praise them."

Comparing these Commandments with the laws of other religions, he observes that theft, adultery, lying, and the destruction of human life (with exceptions), are regarded as sins by all people; that intoxication is only forbidden by Buddhists, Brahmins, and Mahometans, and that the destruction of life, other than human, is regarded as sin by none but Buddhists and Brahmins, believers in the Buddh Avatar. The sanctity of animal life and the use of animal food first claim attention :—

"It is to be observed that animals are agitated, tremble, feel sorrow, show jealousy, and

envy, and fear death, much as men do. Their
existence cannot be compared with that of
plants or trees. We know not whether they
will after death have another existence or not.
But those persons who do believe in another
birth in some greater or lesser world, who believe in transmigration, must believe that it is
sinful to kill any animal. He who is merciful
and compassionate and believes in the cer-
tainty of future existences, will not venture to
kill or shorten the life of any being from compassion and fear of the consequences.

"Question. If then he who has compassion
will not injure their lives, why does he support
his life on their flesh? were there no eaters,
there would be no killers. Is not the eating
of flesh sin?

"Answer. There is a Buddhist ordinance
which declares that there is no sin in eating
proper meat, although it is a sin to cause the
death of animals. With respect to this argument, we observe that those who hold the
slaughter of animals to be sinful are few compared with those who believe that there is no
harm in it. Supposing that those who are compassionate were to refuse to eat meat, others

would kill and trade in it and the animals
would die. The Mahometans do not eat pork,
so pigs ought to abound in their countries, but
in fact there are none at all. Animals must
die by the law of nature, nor will the absence
of any one to eat them prevent their death.
The religion of Buddha does not compel any to
act against their own dispositions, it only indi-
cates good and evil.

"When on a present of meat being made,
the receiver expresses his great pleasure, says
that he has been longing for that kind of meat,
and orders it to be cooked at once, and makes
it clear to the giver that he wishes for more,
and so incites him to go and kill more, this is
unrighteous. Again, when one insists on one's
servants getting some kind of meat which one
knows they will not find ready killed in the
market, and so forces them to have some spe-
cially killed, this is uncompassionate and
wicked. If a monk knows in any way that
animals are killed merely to supply him with
flesh, he should abstain from that flesh; it is
impure and the laws of the priesthood forbid
him to eat it.

"The Lord Buddha was asked to forbid

animal food, but he would not. There are those who hold his religion, but will not accept the first commandment, like the Chinese, who believe in transmigration as Buddhists, but assert that there is no sin in executing criminals or in killing animals for food."

Next, as to the vice of intoxication.

"As to the sin of drinking intoxicating things, consider! It is a cause of the heart becoming excited and overcome. By nature there is already an intoxication in man caused by desire, anger, and folly; he is already inclined to excess, and not thoughtful of death, sorrow, and the instability of things. If we stimulate this natural intoxication by drinking, it will become more daring; and if the natural inclination is to anger, anger will become excessive, and acts of violence and murder will result. Similarly with the other inclinations. The drunken man neither thinks of future retribution nor present punishment.

"Again, spirituous liquors cause disease, liver disease, and short life; and the use of them when it has become a habit cannot be dispensed with without discomfort, so that men spend all their money unprofitably in purchasing them, and when their money is spent become thieves and dacoits. The evil is both future and immediate."

He refers to the Total Abstinence Movement and the Mahometan law thus :—

" In the present age, many Americans have declared spirit-drinking to be an evil, a cause of much immediate mischief, and of no future good. The Jews used not to consider spirit-drinking a sin, but Mahomet declared that Allah had ordered him to forbid its use, on the ground that spirit-drinkers, if they went to heaven, would smell so offensively that the angels could not endure their vicinity."

On the subject of the third commandment, we are told that women who are the objects of another's jealous care, that is, wives and unmarried women, who are cared for or supported by their husbands or relatives, and women who are betrothed, are all improper objects of desire ; but as this is " the undisputed opinion of all except those bad men who think there is no harm in adultery unless it is discovered," the main point considered is, why under this commandment men and women are put on a different footing, that is, why polygamy is allowed ?

" If we say the commandment is different for men and women, we make two commands of it ; but it is not so, it is only one, an order that sensual intercourse should be suitably regulated.

" Women are not allowed to have more than one husband, because they are under the rule of man, and not superior to man. If women might have many husbands, they would not know who was the father of their children, and these children might injure, and even commit parricide, without knowing it. And, moreover, the dipositions of men and women differ ; men, however many wives they have, and whatever their liking or dislike to any of them, have no desire to kill them ; but if women had more husbands than one, they would wish to kill all but the one they liked best, for such is their nature. There are many stories in point, one of which I will relate concisely.

" There was once on a time a priest who daily blessed a great king, saying ' May your Majesty have the perseverance of a crow, the daring of a woman, the endurance of a vulture, and the strength of an ant.' And the king, doubting his meaning, said ' What do you

mean by the endurance of a vulture?' and he
replied, 'If a vulture and all kinds of other
animals are caged up without food, the vulture will outlive them all.' And the king tried,
and it was so. And the priest said, 'I spoke
of the strength of the ant, for an ant is
stronger than a man, or anything that lives.
No other animal can lift a lump of iron or
copper as large as itself, but an ant will carry
off its own bulk of either metal, if it be only
smeared with sugar. And I said 'the perseverance of the crow,' for none can subdue the
boldness and energy of the crow; however long
you cage it, you will never tame it. And if
the king would see the daring of a woman,
I beg him to send for a couple who have been
married only one or two months, who are yet
deeply in love with one another, and first call
the husband, and say, "Go and cut off your
wife's head, and bring it to me, and I will
give you half my kingdom, and make you my
viceroy." And if he will not do it, then send
for the woman, and say, "Kill your husband,
and bring me his head, and I will make you
my chief queen, ruler of all the ladies in the
palace." And the king did so. He found a

newly-married couple who had never quarrelled, and were deeply enamoured of one another, and sending for the husband, he spoke to him as the priest had suggested. And the man took the knife, and hid it in his dress, and that same night rose when his wife slept, thinking to kill her, but he could not, because he was kind-hearted, and reflected that she had done no wrong. And the next day he returned the knife to the king, saying that he could not use it against his wife. Then the king sent messengers to the wife secretly, and they brought her to him, and he flattered and enticed her with promises, as the priest had told him, and she took the knife, and as soon as her husband slept, stabbed him, and cut off his head, and took it to the king. This story shows not only that woman is more daring than man, but also that if any one entices and pleases them, they will plot their husband's death, which is a good reason for not letting them have more than one husband.

"At the time Jesus Christ lived, and still later in Mahomet's time, there was no law of monogamy. Mahomet limited the number of wives to four, and after a time Europeans instituted monogamy by law, not from religious motives, but from conviction of its expediency, considering that plurality of wives was unfair to women, and gave rise to jealousy and murder and constant trouble.

" The religion of Buddha highly commends a life of chastity. Buddha stated that when a man could not remain as a celibate, if he took but one wife it was yet a kind of chastity, a commendable life. Buddha also censured polygamy as involving ignorance and lust, but he did not absolutely forbid it, because he could not say there was any actual wrong in a man having a number of wives properly acquired."

Polygamy is extensively practised in Siam, the kings setting the example. The late king's life affords an instance of both celibacy and polygamy. At the age of twenty his majesty, who had been already married for some years, entered the priesthood and remained a monk for twenty-seven years; he then came to the throne, and accepting the custom of polygamy as suitable for his new position, he was within the next sixteen years blessed with a family of seventy-nine children. The number of his wives we could not ascertain. Many noblemen have thirty or forty or more wives. So far as our own observation goes, this polygamy, accompanied by a facility for divorcement, is not attended by very evil results. There is a great deal of domestic happiness in Siam, and suicides and husband and wife murders, so common in monogamic Europe, are rare there. Nevertheless, many of the best men we have known there were theoretical admirers of monogamy, and one practised it.

Having thus treated of morality and charity, we might expect our author to discourse on the nature of meditation, which is the great Buddhistic means of self-improvement. We presume that he omits it because it is only practised by monks, whilst his book is intended for laymen. In the absence of any remarks from him, we will only observe that by meditation and self-abstraction from all human concerns and passions, Buddhists believe man can purify himself, and can attain supernatural knowledge and power, and ultimately perfection.

We now revert to the nature of future existence. Firstly we have a sketch of the ideas of Christians, Mahometans, and Brahmins, as to a future life, heaven and hell, which we need not quote, but pass to his exposition of the Buddhist views.

"In the religion of Phra Somana Kodom we also find mention of heaven and hell, and we are taught that those who have kept the Commandments, given alms, and lived righteously, will after death go to heavenly palaces furnished with houris, more or less numerous, according to the amount of merit they have acquired. And those who have no merit, but have only acquired demeritorious Kam, will on death go to hell, and remain there until their Kam is exhausted, when they will be born again as animals or men; or if there is any merit still belonging to them, they may even go to heaven. Those whose merit has caused them to be born as angels in heaven will, when the power of their merit is exhausted, be extinguished in heaven, and reappear as men or animals, or sometimes, when a demeritorious Kam still attaches to them, they will fall to hell. There is no fixity, but continual circulation and alternation, until such time as the spirit has become perfect in 'the four ways and

the four fruits,'* which extinguish all further
sorrow, stay all further change, and cause
eternal rest in a state of perfect happiness
where there is no further birth, nor old age,
nor death. Even those who do not believe in
the religion of Buddha, by good actions acquire
merit, and will on their death attain heaven,
and by evil actions acquire demerit, and on
death will pass to hell. Buddhism does not
teach the necessary damnation of those who do
not believe in Buddha, and in this respect I
think it is more excellent than all the other religions which teach that all but their own followers will surely go to hell."

After remarking that women as well as men
can enjoy the highest pleasures of heaven, and
that there may be a change of sex with a
change of state, he gives his own views of the
common sensual idea of heaven.

"The fact of the matter is this. The Hin-
doos who live in countries adjoining the Mahometan countries believe that in heaven every

* These are the four highest grades of sanctity. He
who attains the first will reach Nippan within seven
existences; the fourth leads to Nippan direct, without
any existence intervening.

male has tens and hundreds of thousands of female attendants, according to what their teachers of old taught them concerning the riches of heaven, and their idea is akin to that of the Mahometans. The Mahometans had held out great inducements, representing the pleasures that would result from their religion; and the Hindoo teachers, fearing that their people might be excited by this most promising new doctrine, themselves introduced it into their own teaching. At least, this is my impression on the subject. But if we must speak out the truth as to these matters, we must say that the world of heaven is but similar to the world of man, only differing in the greater amount of happiness there enjoyed. Angels there are in high places with all the apparel and train of their dignity, and others of lower station with less surroundings. All take up that position which is due to their previous merits and demerits. Buddha censured concupiscence; Buddha never spoke in praise of heaven; he taught but one thing as worthy of praise, 'the extinction of sorrow.' All this incoherent account of heaven is but the teaching of later writers, who have preached the luxuries and rich pleasures of heaven in hopes thereby to attract men into the paths of holiness, and the attainment of sanctity. We cannot say where heaven and earth are. All religions hold that heaven is above the world and hell below it, and every one of them uses heaven to work on men's desires, and hell to frighten them with. Some hold forth more horrors than others, according to the craft of those who have designed them to constrain men by acting on their fears, and making them quake and tremble. We cannot deny the existence of heaven and hell, for as some men in this world certainly live well and others live ill, to deny the existence of heaven and hell would be to deprive men's works of their result, to make all their good deeds utterly lost to them. We must observe, that after happiness follows sorrow, after heat follows cold; they are things by nature coupled. If after death there is a succession of existence, there must be states of happiness and of sorrow, for they are necessarily coupled in the way I have explained. As for heaven being above the earth and hell below it, I leave intelligent people to come to their own conclusion; but as to future states of happiness and sorrow, I feel no doubt whatever."

He next remarks, "That both in ancient and modern times there have been instances of persons who, on recovering from a state of trance, have declared that they have visited other worlds during their trance." We quote one of his modern instances :—

"A young Cambodian, aged eighteen, living at the hamlet of Phrakanong, in Siam, being sick of fever, swooned for a day and then recovered animation. On recovery he said, 'that he had been bound and taken to a place where there were a number of seething frying-pans containing oil or water, he was not sure which, and crowds of men and women were being unceasingly hurried along and thrown into the frying-pans, but they rejected him, saying that he had been brought there by mistake, and they drove him back to his own place."

Some observations on the disposal of the bodies of the dead appropriately follow. "This," he writes, "is not a religious question, though Christians, in preferring burial, do look to rising in their own bodies at the sound of the trumpet when God shall come to judge them, but it is a matter of custom and convenience." The Siamese practise "cremation, a rite derived by the Buddhists from the Brahmins," and he approves it, as causing less pollution of air and water than burial does.

The concluding pages of the 'Kitchanukit' are chiefly repetitions of what has gone before. We shall then conclude our notice with the following extract :—

"How can it be according to the belief of those who believe in but one resurrection, who believe in a man being received into heaven while his nature is still full of impurity, by virtue of sprinkling his head with water, or cutting off by circumcision a small piece of his skin? Will such a man be purified by the merit of the Lord Allah, or of Thao Maha Phrom? We know not where they are. We have never seen them. But we do know and can prove that men can purify their own natures, and we know the laws by which that purification can be effected. Is it not better to believe in this which we can see and know, than in that which has no reality to our perceptions?"

Such are the ideas and arguments of an honest and earnest Buddhist of the present day, defending his religion against the assaults of the numerous body of missionaries who live in comfort, and teach without molestation among his countrymen. He is indebted to them for much information, and willingly accepts it. He listens to and admires the morality of the Christian religion, until they believe him almost a Christian, and then he tells them that Buddha too taught a morality as beautiful as theirs, and a charity that extends to everything that has breath. And when they speak of faith, he answers that by the light of the knowledge they have helped him to, he can weed out his old superstitions, but that he will accept no new ones. Their cause is, as the late king said, hopeless :—

"You must not think that any of my party will ever become Christians. We will not embrace what we think is a foolish religion."

The religion of Buddha meddled not with the Beginning, which it could not fathom; avoided the action of a Deity it could not perceive; and left open to endless discussion that problem which it could not solve, the ultimate reward of the perfect. It dealt with life as it found it; it declared all good which led to its sole object, the diminution of the misery of all sentient beings; it laid down rules of conduct which have never been surpassed, and held out reasonable hopes of a future of the most perfect happiness.

Its proofs rest on the assumptions that the reason of man is his surest guide, and that the law of nature is perfect justice. To the disproof of these assumptions, we recommend the attention of those missionaries who wish to convert Buddhists.

II. A.

www.ingramcontent.com/pod-product-compliance
Lightning Source LLC
Chambersburg PA
CBHW032248080426
42735CB00008B/1055